Fern Plumb

Vital Possessions

Vital Possessions

GRACE NOLL CROWELL

ABINGDON PRESS   NEW YORK—NASHVILLE

VITAL POSSESSIONS

Copyright © 1960 by Abingdon Press

Library of Congress Catalog Card Number: 60-10908

SET UP, PRINTED, AND BOUND BY THE
PARTHENON PRESS, AT NASHVILLE,
TENNESSEE, UNITED STATES OF AMERICA

Dedication

To all those who value God's manifold **and** marvelous bestowals, deeming them important and priceless, as they are, I dedicate this **book** most sincerely

Preface

If any reader of this little book should, through that reading, become more conscious of his vital spiritual possessions, I shall be humbly grateful.

Surely those possessions are many and precious and should be deeply cherished, thus pleasing the Giver of all good.

GRACE NOLL CROWELL

Contents

Vital Possessions

God's Gifts to Man

Dawn, with its platinum silver, and the sun
Come unfailingly from the open hand of God:
His first gift of the day to warm the heart
And bathe with beauty all the earth's
   green sod.

Noon and its pure gold, set like some gem
Above the world—a light sent on its way
To draw the seeded earth's good substance up
Enriching the harvesting for which we pray.

God dips his hand in glory, spreads it far
As the sun goes down within the crimson west.
Before such splendor men should stand in awe
And lift a reverent heart within the breast.

The universe is steadied by the hand
That gives these precious gifts
   of nights and days.
God grant we may not fail to render thanks
And prove our gratitude by heartfelt praise.

1

OUR BIBLE

*And Jesus answered him, saying, It is written,
That man shall not live by bread alone, but
by every word of God.*　　LUKE 4:4

WE MAY BE ASSURED THAT THE CHRISTIAN
today has absolute right to claim the eternal
truths of the Bible. God spread his word before
us, pointing the way to go, and he maps out
definitely the destination we will reach if we
follow his clear directives.

The Bible is ours. It is our most valuable possession. We claim it as our own, and we have
the right to all the promises made therein. We
have every reason to heed the admonitions given
us for our good, knowing that God's will for
us is always best, always right.

Christians have ever valued and cherished
the Book and have striven to follow its teach-

ings, and they will continue to do so while the world lasts.

We think of our forefathers who, centuries ago, knowing it was necessary for their own souls' good, and for that of their children, broke with the old regime and went to a new and untried land in order to be free to worship their God as they would. It was a monumental and momentous decision that they were forced to make. In many ways their lives in the old country were easier than they would be in the new land, but these stalwart folk put God first in their daily living. There they were being continually oppressed and coerced in their worship, and their hearts were gravely troubled.

There came a day when the decision must be made. They were to find passage on a small, fragile ship, and they learned that so few of their household goods could be taken aboard that they were dumbfounded.

We think of one family—the husband and father, a carpenter, who did beautiful work with tools. The family's livelihood depended upon the income brought in by the use of those tools—and now most of them must be left behind. It was a grave situation, but in his little workshop he took up one beloved tool after another. A saw must go with him, the hammer was an absolute necessity, perhaps the chisel. These three would be needed desperately in the building of a new home in the vast wilderness where they were going. So discarding the other strong, steel implements, he chose the three.

His good wife was in the kitchen endeavoring to select the few things she would be permitted to carry with her. Surely she must take a good, stout knife, a sharp-tined fork, an iron kettle— no woman could keep house with less. And so these three were chosen.

The children, in great excitement, were clamoring about her, endeavoring, with her help, to select among their simple, homemade toys the most beloved one. Each was permitted to take but one, and to a child's heart it was a distressful situation.

Finally the selections were made, and the father and mother looked at each other. There was one more decision—one more of their possessions to go with them that must not, could not, be left behind.

There on a small table lay the great family Bible, beautiful in workmanship, sturdily bound in cured leather, fortified with brass clasps and hinged back. This must go if all else be left behind. To be sure it was heavy, but it would be their compass on a wild and stormy sea. It would be their stay and comfort in a strange, untested land, and they would need its guidance—every word of it.

Said the husband to the wife, "We will trust God for our daily bread in the new land, but our Lord plainly says: 'Man cannot live by bread alone but by every word of God.'" And there in the little home, for the last time, they and their children knelt and prayed for guidance, for wisdom and strength during the precarious journey ahead, and for his protective care over them in the new homeland.

They wrapped the Bible carefully in burlap and carried it with them: a possession from which they never were parted.

Years later their children's children, a western-looking people, went through the same procedure of selection. A covered wagon could hold little more of a family's worldly goods than did the small ship. Some things must be discarded, some taken, and they too chose to take the old family Bible, beloved for years and worn from much usage. It was their map by which to travel on earth—their chart on their heavenward journey.

The prairie schooners creaked and groaned and headed into the sunset, and these men and women—those future empire builders—making their way across trackless wastes—would pause at late evening, build their glowing campfires, and take the Bible from its stout covering. There they would commit their way unto the Lord, consulting with him through his word, inquiring the way to go, and proceeding on the morrow to live "not by bread alone," but by God's answering voice.

They took his promises and made them their own. The long, weary journey was made less weary by the hope garnered from the good Book the evening before. They had laid claims to the promises made to the righteous ones long ago. It was their heritage, and they hoarded that heritage gratefully in their hearts as they moved forward on their westward journey.

Today we, too, are pioneers in a sense. We find ourselves in a new and untried world. What shall we as pilgrims and strangers carry with us in our hearts on our forward going? Should not our best equipment be the much-read, much-loved word of God, without which we are lost in any hitherto untraversed land—lost in trackless wastes of the world's dilemma? There is no way out, save through obedience to that word, no way but his way. Let us make no mistake about it.

Forever There Is God

In the beginning God, and in between
And throught the vast forever there is God.
We can see his mighty handwork if we look,
And if we scan the pathway man has trod,
We can mark his footprints traveling close
    beside
The weary and bewildered ones of earth.
We hear the gentle voice upon the wind
Of him who is our comrade from our birth.

In the beginning he created light
That we may walk unhindered down the
    land.
He made us in his image, gave his Word
So clear that any heart can understand.
Though all else fail, this light will never
    dim
Along the way for those who walk with
    him.

2

THE CHURCH

> *Now therefore ye are no more strangers and
> foreigners, but fellow-citizens with the
> saints, and of the household of God; And
> are built upon the foundation of the apostles
> and prophets, Jesus Christ himself being the
> chief corner stone; In whom all the build-
> ing fitly framed together groweth unto an
> holy temple in the Lord.* EPH. 2:19-21

WHAT A BLESSED FELLOWSHIP! WHAT AN
honorable citizenship is ours who love the church
with an unwavering devotion! What a marvelous corner stone and how firm the rock-bound
foundation on which it rests!

The old hymn that has been sung by countless thousands through the years emphasizes
the firmness and indestructibility of the foundation upon which all orthodox churches are
built. It declares:

> The Church's one foundation
> Is Jesus Christ her Lord;
> She is His new creation
> By water and the word:
> From heaven He came and sought her
> To be His holy bride,
> With His own blood He bought her,
> And for her life He died.

We read in his word that the foundation is set so deeply in the Rock of Ages that even the gates of hell shall not, cannot, prevail against it. This word has been proved true even though we know that in the hell of war many individual churches were blown to bits, but their foundations remained, and new churches slowly but surely arose upon those structures, their steepled fingers pointing skyward to call men's minds to the truth of the holy word.

It is strange that in the four Gospels the word church is mentioned but three times, and those are in Matt. 16:18 and 18:17. However, the organized church was not born until the fiftieth day after the passover, when the Holy Spirit descended upon the faithful waiting ones who were heeding their Lord's command to "Tarry in Jerusalem until ye be endued with power from on high."

They obeyed. They waited patiently with faith, and when the Holy Spirit descended upon them, they were filled with a strange, dynamic power hitherto unknown. It was then that the church became "the fellowship of the spirit" and "the body of Christ."

God's people were "no longer strangers and foreigners on the earth, but fellow citizens in the household of God."

The Church then became a growing power that nothing can surpass nor destroy. The evil rulers of the world are striving to batter down its doors, to smother it with the dust of their frenzied fury, but they cannot shake its rock-locked foundation nor permanently destroy the "holy temple" of the Lord.

All things and all people belong to God, and he has given his Son, Jesus Christ, to be the head, the chief and supreme corner stone of the living church, it having no other ruler save the Christ.

Therefore, as we enter its doors, if we are attentive and reverent, we are made definitely aware of his presence—in the aisles, in the pews, in the pulpit. And our worship will be more profound, more sincere as we feel that motivating power working in our midst.

The living church is a Christian's vital possession, for as soon as one becomes a member, that church is his. It belongs to him, and it belongs to me. It is as much mine as if I had bought and paid for it.

"My church." I say the words reverently as one says, "My Lord and my God," or "My home, my country." The church whose builder and maker is God. I say it with awe. I marvel at the significance of the statement, at the wealth of my heritage.

My church! Here I was reborn. Here I came when very young and learned to love Jesus. My tender heart took upon it his image so clearly that all the dust of the years has not been able to obscure that picture: the gentle shepherd seeking the little lost, shivering lamb, the loving Jesus welcoming the children into his open arms, the master, stilling, the wild tempest. Thus the pictures, like continuous films, were photographed upon my heart and mind indelibly. Very early in the church I learned that I belong to Jesus, and that he belongs to me. Here I was baptized in the name of the Father and the Son and the Holy Spirit, with clear water that is the symbol of all purity. Here I found food for my spirit in the words of the minister of my church.

I dine well on the food he has prayerfully prepared for me. Here I bring the first fruits of my earnings and rejoice to return them to the giver of all good who has ever amazed me by the blessings he has poured out upon me—the blessings he has promised all who will bring the tithes into the storehouse.

Here I come to the table which is spread with the emblems of Jesus' broken body and his blood. I partake of them reverently in remembrance of him who died for me. Here I repeat again and again my creed, which is a heritage handed down to me from the early Christians, fresh from their strange and vital experiences.

Here I was married. The tall, white candles at any altar are no whiter than were the holy desires in my heart to be worthy of that new-found, all-enveloping happiness.

It was in the midweek prayer service that I learned to lift a shy voice in prayer and become strengthened thereby. I found in these meetings the courage to stand and give my simple and sincere testimony of God's everlasting goodness to me, and I was freed from fear as I found that a church group is inherently kind and not critical of another's faltering attempts at expression. Here I was carried to the very gates of heaven on the wings of a lifting anthem, I have been reassured and blessed through the singing of the old, loved hymns in which I joined.

Here I have come in sorrow, and I have found comfort in the quietness of my pew where God speaks to me, and in the sympathy and understanding love of the dear friends in my church —for truly here I have found my truest and most faithful friends.

Being a pilgrim and a stranger here on earth and having no continuing city, I have often of necessity had to have my letter moved, but whatever church I join, be it old or new, large or small, it at once becomes my church. It is my Father's house, and I am at home there. Those I meet beneath its roof are my brothers and sisters whom I love, and who, I believe, love me.

Someday I shall have to leave an earthly

church for the last time. The shining thing that is my spirit will have departed on a far journey, and my friends may gather and perhaps be a bit sorrowful for a while that I will no longer be in their midst, but it will only be another move, my last, and to a city that will be my final dwelling place.

Rest assured I shall carry my letter with me from the church militant to the church triumphant and eternal in the heavens. I have no doubt of my reception there, and so I say it over again, slowly, reverently, "My church." And the depth of its meaning increases as I repeat the words, "My church! Thank God for my church."

The Pointing Steeple

Pointing its steeple to the azure sky
Like an earnest pleading voice, like a lifted cry,
The church stands close beside a city street,
Bidding the great throngs stay their hurrying feet,
Bidding all hurt ones lose their weight of care,
And looking heavenward, lift their voice in prayer
To One who bids them come to him for rest.
His promise is to come at his behest
And their heavy-laden hearts that seek release
Can find within God's house his promised peace.
The call is crystal-clear—give heed, O men.
The voice is as compelling now as when
The Christ moved out across the earth's worn sod,
Calling to men to take their way to God.
Oh, today may the whole bewildered hurt world
   turn
And find the blessed peace for which they yearn.

3

HOMES

> *And Jesus saith unto him, The foxes have*
> *holes, and the birds of the air have nests;*
> *but the Son of man hath not where to lay*
> *his head.* MATT. 8:2

THE HOMELESS CHRIST! IN ALL THE HOLY WRIT
there is no more pathetic and heart-breaking
statement than that of the above text.

It is good to know that in his childhood and
early manhood our Lord had an exceptionally
happy and peace-filled life in the little Nazareth
home.

His mother was the one chosen out of the
whole earth by the heavenly Father to mother
his only begotten Son. The beautiful, consecrated young woman, whose spiritual qualifica-
tions were of the highest and purest, made a
home for her family where peace and contentment had their permanent abode. She made it a

gracious, livable place to meet a growing family's needs.

Truly, Mary was one of the women to whom King Solomon referred so eloquently. For she was "a virtuous woman whose price was far above rubies," one whose husband trusted and loved her implicitly.

She "worked diligently" for the good of her household. She arose to prepare the needed food for those she loved. She stretched forth her hands to the poor and needy; she opened her mouth with wisdom, and her tongue spoke kindly. Her children rose up and "called her blessed," and her husband praised her. She was a woman who loved her Lord and obeyed him. Surely she deserved the highest possible honor and praise.

Joseph, Jesus' foster father, was a man of absolute integrity and sterling worth. His tender care over his family was like a warm, enveloping cloak. He reared the first born with the same wise devotion that he gave to his own sons later on.

We know that he taught Jesus his own practical and honorable trade, and that he greatly valued his aptitude as an assistant in the skilled handling of the beautiful, grained wood and the sharp, gleaming tools. And Jesus must have been a constant source of surprise and joy to him as he smoothly turned out a yoke, a table, a bed, or a chair.

The little home was admirably situated for the good of a growing family: a quiet village with nearby neighbors who were well acquainted with Mary and Joseph's eldest son, Jesus, that model of virtue and goodness. Doubtless they held him up to their own sons as a shining example of courteous behavior.

The countryside surrounding Nazareth was admirably situated. The desert was near enough so that the lad could watch the weaving lines of the caravans taking their constant way on matters of trade, and there was a mountain close enough to which he could walk and climb. He could view the blue Mediterranean Sea, sparkling in the far distance. There he could stand and behold on all sides the outstretching landscape and meditate on the world "and the fullness thereof." The beauty that unfolded before him must, to his sensitive nature, have been so intense that it was akin to pain.

In that little Nazareth home his first thirty years were spent and his teaching mission began.

But, alas, he went forth with no place to lay his dear head!

It was not strange that he often sought the home of his friends, Lazarus and Martha and Mary. How greatly he must have enjoyed their kindly hospitality! Even little, humble Zacchaeus, to whose home he invited himself at mealtime, no doubt meant a pleasant interlude to our Lord as he labored among the throngs that so constantly beseiged him.

Our God values home life so greatly that he set mankind in families.

No doubt Jesus was glad that even the wild life about him was more fortunate than he, that they had their snug dens, their protective nests for their needs and their comfort.

The dictionary defines the word *home* as "a dwelling place, a place of affection." This is an apt definition for any true home. Where Christ is an abiding guest, a home ever holds the deep affection of its possessors.

It matters not whether it be the flat-roofed, mud-daubed house of Jesus' day or the more modern construction of today, a home is a home the world over since time began, and will continue to be while it lasts.

33

Back in the early part of this century, Adelina Patti, the famous concert artist, sang one night to a large audience in one of our great cities. Her voice, clear and strong and sweet, welled up with power as she sang the classics, but for her closing number she chose to sing the simple, well-known, well-loved "Home Sweet Home." Clear, harmonious, resonant, her voice lifted in the melody of the song, ending with the appealing lines:

> Be it ever so humble
> There is no place like home.

The classics had been thoroughly enjoyed, but as the singer bowed and turned to leave the stage, the vast audience rose in a body, and the ovation was tremendous.

The singer had sung their song—a song that belonged to each one individually. A home, a true home, is an universal passion in the heart of mankind, and the great throng could not remain silent under that homage.

The word *home* brings each of us the thought of the home we now occupy or the memory of some earlier one that had been a shelter and protection against the storms of life.

I think of my own home with the peculiar tenderness we all feel for our own dwelling places. Mine is not a grand house as houses go. It is old and marred with scars, but it stands on a quiet, terraced street with a huge Magnolia tree in the rear as background. The tree is filled with the bright activity of birds and the soft whispering of winds. At its side stands an ancient pear tree, which is adorned in the spring like a white-clothed bride, and in the autumn it brings forth its golden fruit lavishly.

The walls of my house hold memories that sound in my heart like faint, far-away music, and the house is precious beyond price, for it is that wonderful thing men call "home."

To be sure its bricks are not as pristine as they once were. The woodwork needs paint, for which it will have to wait, and the foundation has sagged somewhat. The thresholds bear evidence of much going out and coming in, but the rooms still echo with the laughter of children who have been long since grown up. The sound of voices of many a beloved guest echoes there, while the whole house is vibrant with the stirring of present and pleasant everyday living.

Home, the pulse beat of the ages, lives deeply

hidden within its meaning. I know of no other word that has the power to break the heart with soul-shaking nostalgia as does this one word. To be sure, one must be away from home to fully experience this indescribable illness. And yet let certain songs be loosed upon the air, and one may suddenly feel the intolerable ache of nostalgia. Tears will well up unbidden as one thinks of the homeless ones of earth, and the longing to relieve that deep hurt will burn passionately within the breast.

I have experienced many things, but I have never known but joy in any homecoming. I round the corner after long journeying and spy my own chimney, reddened by the sunset. The windows will be glittering with the gold of that last pure light, and suddenly I am there, my feet quick and ringing upon the walk, my hand reaching to turn the key. I catch the faint, sweet scent of the hardy perennials in my neighbor's garden, and I breathe the fragrance of my own four o'clocks. A neighbor across the way calls out her glad welcoming, and I am home! In all the world is there anything better than this?

Thank God for home—for my home and for

every home where Christ and love abide. There is a peculiar tenderness in the love of a family one for another, of parents for their children, of children for their parents. Surely, concentrated love is like the light that "shines more and more unto the perfect day."

It humbles me to be the recipient of this great unmerited favor, for who can fully be worthy of the marvelous things the name *home* implies? Home is that gift direct from the outgiving hand of God. Out of the earth he has created have come the brick and mortar and the sturdy timbers which enter into the building of even the simplest home, and they are blest by the One who had no home to call his own! Yet he planned that we, who are not always deserving, should be comfortably housed and sheltered.

It is his blueprint straight from heaven. May we keep his plan unchanged on earth. May we make, and keep, Christ the head of our households—that by his precept and example we may be better housekeepers here and thus become more worthy to inherit the mansions which belong to our heavenly Father and which are to be his legacy to us as our future eternal home.

A Gift from Heaven

A sheltering roof, a hearth stone,
A table neatly laid
In a home, since its beginning,
Where the gracious Christ has stayed
To direct and guide a family
That turns to him in need;
This is a gift from heaven,
A blessed gift, indeed.

A place where hearts are shielded
From the world's wild, restless din,
Where love is a benediction,
And peace can enter in.
Surely no other structure,
That lifts from the earth's dark loam,
Can bless and comfort the spirit
As does a house called *Home*.

4

OUR COUNTRY

> *And it shall come to pass, if thou shalt hearken diligently unto the voice of the Lord thy God, to observe and to do all his commandments . . . that the Lord thy God will set thee on high above all nations of the earth.* DEUT. 28:1

FAR BACK IN THE OLD TESTAMENT WE FIND almost a reiteration of the above text, admonishing a nation, bidding its people how to live in order to have their hurt land healed and blessed:

If my people, which are called by my name, shall humble themselves, and pray, and seek my face, and turn from their wicked ways; then will I hear from heaven, and will forgive their sins, and will heal their land. (II Chr. 7:14.)

It is surely time that our nation heeds these admonitions. Surely it is high time!

Borne upon the air comes the sound of voices, like an anthem lifted heavenward. Beautifully, these words ring out:

> Blessed shalt thou be in the city,
> and blessed shalt thou be in the field.
>
> .   .   .   .
>
> Blessed shall be thy basket and thy store.
> Blessed shalt thou be when thou comest in,
> and blessed shalt thou be when thou goest out.
> (Deut.28:3, 5-6.)

And again the promise: "The Lord shall establish thee an holy people unto himself, as he hath sworn unto thee, if thou shalt keep the commandments . . . , and walk in his ways." (Deut. 28:9.)

This is straight, stark, simple language that we in America, who love our land, would indeed be wise to heed. If America is ever to be set high above all nations, it will not be because of any geographical advantage or any unusual wealth she may possess, but because we, as a people, are willing and eager to meet God's unqualified conditions.

If the Lord is to establish us as a holy people unto himself, we must "walk in his ways." This is the only way that any nation can long survive. God grant that we in America may lay hold of the privilege that is ours: to serve, to obey, to follow the living Christ so closely that we may, through him, become a light for all the world to see.

We grow serious, and indeed earnest, when we consider the importance of our nation to us and to the rest of the world. We have a vast responsibility as citizens in its welfare.

Too often we have been indifferent and careless, going our heedless way, but today, with our liberty upon the chess boards of the world, it may well be that we will at last grow serious.

"My country, 'tis of thee . . ." How many countless times have we lifted our voices in singing the old patriotic hymn, with our minds elsewhere! They were meandering minds. We sang with no thought at all of the strong and beautiful words.

> Land where my fathers died,
> Land of the pilgrims' pride . . .

The land, we felt, was taking care of itself. It

was not our concern, not our responsibility. But now, when danger threatens, we are like children whose mother has become seriously ill. We are apt to panic. We regret bitterly our careless taking-for-granted attitude. A new fierce concern burns in our hearts, and we pray earnestly to God to spare her life, to give us wisdom to do our part in the healing of this grave illness.

Our country, so long taken for granted, has become a vital factor in our lives. We are serious and sincere now as we sing:

> My country, 'tis of thee,
> Sweet land of liberty . . .

It is our country now. It is a beautiful, free land whose life itself has been endangered. It is a never-never land to many of the peoples of the earth; a land of splendor where we, the inhabitants, go walking along pathways of radiance and light, with cornucopias spilling their bright fruits at our feet and with granaries bursting with golden grain for our taking.

Our country . . . It is truly a beneficent friend, a glorious homeland, a true mother. We visualize her as a great and gracious lady standing beside a shining sea, holding aloft her lamp to light the golden door of entry, offering her bounty to the poor and oppressed as does every true mother of mankind.

We take the far look now as we sing. Our own petty affairs have grown insignificant. We are deeply concerned over the land that has mothered us life long. We lift our hands, and our prayers rise upward like the smoking incense of the evening sacrifice.

> Protect us by Thy might,
> Great God, our King.

We need thy guidance, Lord, knowing that we are unworthy as a people and a nation. We know that only in thy strength can we survive, that implicit obedience to thy law is our salvation. Grant us thy protecting might, Lord, lest we fall.

Softly, within our hearts, we repeat the two brief words over and over, savoring their rich flavor, their magic meaning, their martial music —"Our Country." Our cheeks are wet with overflowing tears, but we let them fall, unashamed.

America

America, America, you hold a sacred trust.
Millions of anxious hearts depend on you
To keep our freedom a staunch, priceless thing,
Which our Fathers, who were brave and true,
Lived for, fought for, died for, that we may
Be free to walk upon the earth today.

America, America, the ominous threat is great.
You have faced so many crises in the past,
And came forth valiantly; your people's lives
Depend on you that freedom still will last.
Pray God that now, as always, we shall stand
A worthy people on unfettered land.

America, America, more precious than fine gold
Is the freedom that has sent our banner high.
A nation prays together that it may
Still lift its undimmed colors on the sky.
God grant our flag may ever stay unfurled
As a symbol of our freedom to the world.

5

NEIGHBORS

> *Which now of these three, thinkest thou,*
> *was neighbour unto him that fell among*
> *the thieves?*   LUKE 10:36

IT IS BLESSED TO THINK OF CHRIST'S CONCERN for the hurt ones of earth and of his approval of those who reach out in mercy to render aid where aid is sorely needed.

We recall the young lawyer who "stood up" and tempted our Lord, asking him what he should do to inherit eternal life. We remember that Jesus said unto him, "What is written in the law?" And how blithely the man responded: "Thou shalt love the Lord thy God with all thy might . . . ; and thy neighbour as thyself." Jesus told him he had answered aright, and said, "This do, and thou shalt live." Then seemingly almost impertinently the young man asked, "Who is my neighbour?"

In reply Jesus told him the interesting parable that has come down to us through the ages for our own guidance. He spoke of the traveler going from Jerusalem to Jericho and how he fell among thieves and was left all but fatally wounded. He told of the supposedly righteous priest who saw the hurt one and who drew his robes about himself and passed by on the other side. Also of the Levite, who, after viewing the wounded man, also went on leaving him to die.

"But a certain Samaritan," he said, "had deep compassion for the man and acted upon it. He bound up his wounds and cared for him, thus saving a life."

"Which now," asked the Lord, "do you think was neighbor to him?" And there could be but one answer. "He that showed mercy."

This parable brings to mind the importance of neighborliness. We think of neighbors we have known in the past and those still near by who have filled a vital place in our lives, often showing us mercy in our need and kindness that helped us through dark days.

We think of them with renewed regard and appreciation, recalling their sterling worth, their free outgiving of themselves to make our days happier and more complete.

I like the sound of the words "my neighbor." It is a friendly sound, a heart-warming and cheering sound. When I think of neighbors, I think of small towns and of little yards so closely aligned that one can scarcely tell where one begins and the other ends.

I think of little homes where men call good-naturedly across to each other, passing the time of day. And where women talk intimately in back yards of their work, their children, and of their brave economies. Surely they are in the strictest sense "close neighbors."

I think also of the widely separated homes down country ways, with the miles of clean, green distance lying between them. And I am sure that wherever there is a house in sight, that house is designated by the friendly term "our neighbor" by those who face toward that abode.

I like to think of lighted lamps at night, glowing warmly across the miles to each other, and it is a comforting sight. For when a man can see another man's home light, friendly and warm, the man is cheered by that light, and when a woman can see another woman's chimney, red against an azure sky, and feels less lonely thereby, these women are neighbors though they see each other but seldom.

There is a warm feeling in my heart for the relationship of neighbors. I like to think of the worn paths that lead from yard to yard and from door to door where neighbors go on errands of mercy and of good will, for hearts need everlasting contact with other hearts. There is no pathway on earth more pregnant with meaning than the paths where neighbors have sought each other in their need.

The world is so large that it is comforting to know that somewhere near us are understanding hearts to which we can turn at any time, and for any need, and there find an unfailing and ready response to our call.

The Bible has something to say about neighbors. It tells us: "Let everyone of us please his neighbour for his good to edification." What improved living there would be if we but heeded this beautiful and gracious consideration one for another!

We are told to love our neighbors as ourselves. Again, what blessedness would ensue from such affection! From the Proverbs come the words:

"For better is a neighbour that is near than the brother far off."

Many of us can testify to that truth. There is a tenderness between those who have lived long side-by-side, sharing each other's joys and sorrows, that is strangely more necessary to our daily living than a relationship that has long been severed by time and distance.

The genuine sympathy that exists between good neighbors when one is in trouble is heartening indeed, and the quick upsurge of rejoicing when good fortune befalls another truly shines "like stars in a dark world."

"Which one thinkest thou is the neighbour?" It is well for us to consider the answer given to that question of long ago. "He that showed mercy."

All around us are the hurt and bewildered ones of earth. We cannot pay our debt to humanity by merely loving our close neighbors— those who love us and are important to our living, although that love is commendable, but we should reach out much farther and love as Christ loves and show mercy as he shows mercy. Then only are we the good neighbors that he had in mind when he set us together as a human family.

Our neighborhood is the whole world today. More and more that fact is borne in upon us. God help us that we may tenderly bind up each other's wounds; God help us to love our fellow men selflessly so that when the Lord comes again and asks the question, "Which one was neighbor to him?" he may, God grant, be referring to us.

"My neighbor . . ." I say it again until it expands in meaning, and, like a pebble cast into the water, it reaches out to encircle and bless the whole waiting and needy world with its beneficence.

My Neighbor

He is my neighbor; he is neighbor to me
Who shows me kindness when my need is sore,
Who proves his sincere neighborliness by making
A smoothly-trodden pathway to my door,
Bringing the joys and sorrows he may bear,
Knowing how sure my sympathy will be,
And who will listen with a tender heart
To any grief that has befallen me.

He is my neighbor down a city square
Or across far reaching prairie lands, who lights
An early lamp and lets its ruddy glow
Be cheering to me on strange lonely nights.
He is my neighbor who speaks no word of scandal
Of other neighbors down a street or lane,
Who answers any call where there is illness,
And whose skilled ministering eases pain.
Bless all women, Lord, and bless each man
Who bears likeness to the good Samaritan.

6

THE UNTRAVERSED
REGIONS

---

*O Lord, how manifold are thy works! in
wisdom has thou made them all, the earth
is full of thy riches.*   ps. 104:24

IN EVERY LIFE THERE ARE VAST UNCHARTED
regions which we, as individuals, do not know
we possess, and there are the manifold works
of God, waiting to be discovered. Great riches
are lying ahead, ready for us to claim and to
use for his glory.

There is wisdom we have lacked, yet which we
can attain through diligent research. There are
treasures that God has kept hidden until man's
need for them becomes imperative. They are
waiting at this very moment to be unearthed.

There are mountain fastnesses to be proved,
the sea's secrets to be revealed, the sky's illimi-

table distance to be understood and evaluated. This all can be accomplished when men realize their limitless capabilities, when they discover their own neglected powers.

So much of our inward beings are vast wastelands. There are countless trails to be blazed in thought and planning that will open up far distances of light and beauty before our dazzled eyes.

There are new roads to be carved through the rock of knowledge. There are valleys to be crossed—perhaps valleys that are dark with threatening storm clouds; yet it is in these that we can often gather strength for the climb ahead.

Awaiting us are adventures for the spirit in these untraversed continents, where a fearless one may grow brave and strong to meet life's eventualities; where a shrinking one can become self-reliant and able to triumph over difficulties; where lonely ones can conquer loneliness and can turn cheerless solitude into a good companionship and that mental wasteland into a fertile field that will yield golden grain for the world's harvest.

The wonder of all this is that as we grow in wisdom and mental stature, we can use common circumstances as stepping stones to higher planes. We can learn to let sorrow send us for consolation to the one true source of all comfort: the unfailing promises of God. We can let disappointments make us realize that they are God's appointments and that some failure that seemingly sets us back in our upward going may in reality lead the way to success.

Every circumstance may be used as a door that will open to a new discovery for our eventual good, that will lead us farther on in the will of God.

Life has not been exhausted for anyone when there are worth-while things to be done—and strength with which to do them. We cannot all be brilliant composers or great artists or gifted poets, yet each of us has his own talents meted out by the hand of God.

We know there is still beautiful music to be written, new art to be perfected, great poetry to be captured and set down on paper. Yet there is always good to be accomplished by the humblest one of us in a troubled and needy world, good that will call out all the reserves in our beings. These reserves are waiting to be summoned if we but listen and heed the call.

There are marvelous, hidden wonders to be sought for, and found, in the word of God—wonders that can open blinded eyes and unstop deaf ears.

There are discoveries to be made in divine love as one realizes the height and depth and breadth of Christ's sacrificial love for us—a love than which there is no greater.

It is high time to explore and to cultivate the hitherto unbroken ground in our hearts and minds. There we will discover fertile soil, new abilities for service to mankind, a depth of sympathy and understanding that we did not know we possessed, an inner strength to bear suffering that has not before been fully tested. There we may find a stronger staff upon which our faith may safely lean, a higher courage than that with which we had formerly been equipped, and a fountain of hope in a ceaseless upward lifting to cheer and comfort our hearts.

Always there will be clear spaces awaiting development to keep us happily occupied. True, we may often find that we must travel through shadowed lowlands of pain and sorrow, but, if we tread them bravely, and if we wait patiently, we will come again into the light. There is no darkness so deep but that somewhere the rays of God's sunlight will pierce through to dispel the gloom.

Exploring one's inner being for worthy possibilities and capabilities is not introversion in its wrong sense. It is rather a reaching outward and upward in order to develop one's self for the highest possible service to God and to man.

When there are faults and failures, there should be the immediate surgery of God's forgiveness and his understanding love. Where there are strange and beautiful discoveries made, they should be at once be shared with others for their enlightenment and pleasure.

Every day we should forge farther ahead into these untraversed fastnesses. Each hour should draw us nearer to the higher altitudes of the life that God, who planned our lives, would have us live. And with his help we may find ourselves greater and more noble in mind and spirit than we have ever dreamed could be possible.

Since God has all of his riches in store for us, since he made us in his own image, why should we not be Godlike? Why, indeed, should we not grow daily to be more like him who made us in his image?

Discovery

I have discovered a region,
A new land in my heart,
That hitherto went untrodden,
Nor had I had a part
In all the vast resources
That were waiting there for me.
I sought them, and found them
And claimed them gratefully.

For they opened wider vistas
Than I had viewed before:
New riches for the spirit,
New treasures held in store
By the hand of God who bade me
To seek, and I should find.
The new land I discovered
Brought wealth to heart and mind.

7

GOD'S GIFT OF BEAUTY

> *Let the beauty of the Lord our God be upon us: and establish thou the work of our hands . . . ; yea, the work of our hands establish thou it.*   PS. 90:17

THE ABOVE TEXT RELATES TO THE REBUILDING of the temple which the surrounding enemies had destroyed.

The pious Jews had begun the work, and they earnestly besought the Lord not to let that work be demolished. They cried to him: "Let the top stone be laid on with shouting." They longed to get the temple of God rebuilt beautifully and that worship there be fittingly restored. It was their greatest grief that the temple had been destroyed and worship therein had been suspended.

Every true Christian should feel more concern for God's glory than he does for his own temporal affairs. One does not wonder that these men of old prayed that the beauty of the Lord God be upon them and that the work of their hands for his glory be firmly established.

In Zech. 9:17 we read, "For how great is his goodness, and how great is his beauty!" We cannot conceive of that goodness and of that beauty, so all encompassing is his goodness, so blindingly white is his beauty. We too may well pray that they be upon us and upon the work of our hands. Goodness is essential to good workmanship wherever it may be found.

Many times in any fine craftsmanship one can note a perfection that is beyond human skill. A perfect statue carved from pure white marble by a great artist bears the mark of a greater power than his own, if it be a breath-taking thing of beauty. Certain music that lives on and on through time and in the heart has God back of it.

We watch a man plowing his level acres, and we are conscious that God is in partnership with him in that labor. The plowing and the planting is the man's part—the good earth, the sun, and the rain are God's.

We see a woman moving about her daily household tasks, and as she brings harmony and order out of chaos, her love of God's universal order has a direct bearing upon her work. "Honour and majesty are before him: strength and beauty are in his sanctuary. Give unto the Lord, O ye kindreds of people . . . Give unto the Lord the glory due unto his name . . . O worship the Lord in the beauty of holiness." (Ps. 96:6-9.)

Beauty is a strong and forceful word throughout the Scriptures. Perhaps it is because God, in his passion of creation, spilled so much of it over the earth that he meant for mankind to gather, as they did the manna of old, and to find in it much to sustain life.

He created the orderly universe of sun and moon and stars. He set the beauty of far horizons to shut us in, that it might become more possible for us to be conscious of the nearby splendors of the hills toward which we are to lift our eyes for strength. He gave us valleys with their quiet vistas, their restful shading of light and shadow, the trees with their emerald reachings— all the little nearby treasures that are our possessions, if we care to take them and make them our own.

Personally, I have often wondered at what may seem, in our human limitations, to be wasted beauty—wasted because God has seemingly purposely hidden it in strange, almost inaccessible places.

Here in America, for instance, at the highest peak of the Continental Divide, one can stand in the snowy landscape, and if he looks down and moves the thin layer of snow about his feet, he can find on any summer day small, beautiful flowers clinging to the rocky soil, as if for protection. The chances are great that no human eye will ever behold them, but God was as meticulous in creating their beauty as he is in making an orchid.

Through a microscope one sees small things become large, and in the tiniest blossom is an unbelievable beauty of creation: the perfected stamen, the delicate pistils, the golden pollen, the intricate veining of the petals, until one wonders if God stood on that glorious height and took his mighty power to create a thing so lovely simply for his own enjoyment.

There is another beauty, one among many thousands, and that is the simple beauty of goodness in the human heart, in self-forgetting, in patience through trial and suffering, through loss and grief. Kagawa, the great, selfless Christian of the Orient, makes his most ardent plea: "O God, make me like Christ!" This is a prayer and a dedication. He feels that he is called upon to serve the poor, and his biographer says, "He has set his feet on the thorny path of service," and he has kept them there. He suffers more than it seems any one should suffer, yet his "strength" is truly "made perfect in weakness." His spirit is flooded with light, and he becomes a flaming evangel for God. His earnest heart's cry is fully answered.

Oh, that we all might give God the glory due unto his name, thus worshiping him in the pure, radiant beauty of holiness. We can well believe that he surrounds us with earthly beauty as a fit setting for that worship, forming a sort of sanctuary about us where we may kneel in reverence and thank him for his perfect gifts.

We may be sure that our appreciation of beauty is a form of worship which is highly acceptable to its Creator. He has given us eyes with which to see. He has dipped his brush in gorgeous colors with which to paint the silver dawn, the gold of high noon, the crimson glory of sunset. He has given us ears with which to catch the music of the wind, the sound of bright water rushing over stones, the exquisite songs from little feathered throats that are bursting with the sheer joy of living.

Too often we are oblivious to all earth's ecstasies. If we should see for the first time some of the everyday glories, we no doubt would fall upon our knees in awe and cry aloud our pleasure and gratitude to the giver.

We all value appreciation for any worthwhile thing we do for others. We are made in God's image, his heart is our heart, and he values praise from his children. Often he must think us indifferent to the gifts he bestows on us so freely. But the desert still blossoms; the forest still holds its green glory unnoted; the everlasting hills are there for all to behold who will and gather strength and courage to meet the problems and complexities of life.

It may be that God did create all these for his own delight. We recall, as the newly created earth slipped from his fingers, that he beheld it and called it good. In his great loving heart he must have known that at least some of his children would accept and value that created beauty for the good of their souls.

It would be wise for any true appreciator to make his mind a sort of photographic lens and thereon catch a lasting impression of a lovely thing to hold in lifelong memory.

He Hath Made Everything Beautiful

ECCL. 8:11

Our God made all things beautiful.
The garden of Eden must have been
A marvelous, sparkling, holy place,
Free from riotous weeds and sin.

In the cool of the morning, when he walked
    through
The fresh green grass and noted each flower,
One does not wonder he called it good
And was pleased with his own creative power.

Even today, when men have spoiled
Much of earth's splendor, there still remains
The pristine beauty of light and shade,
The sun and the moon and the clean, bright rains.

Nothing can dim entirely
The gifts he intended for you and me.

8

MEMORY

> *I will speak of the glorious honour of thy*
> *majesty, and of thy wondrous works. . . .*
> *I will declare thy greatness. They shall*
> *abundantly utter the memory of thy great*
> *goodness, and shall sing of thy righteous-*
> *ness.*   PS. 145:5-7

THUS OF THE SPLENDORS HELD IN MEMORY, the psalmist sings to praise and glorify the Lord, and thus would I, one of his humblest singers, speak.

Memory in itself is a musical word with its singing vowels and the depth of its meaning. A richly stored memory in the minds of men is a priceless possession. It is a value to cherish and to fall back upon when days are dark or when the future may look bleak and appalling.

Again the psalmist speaks: "Thy word have I

hid in mine heart, that I might not sin against thee."

That hidden word became a vital memory in his heart. It prevented his sinning before God or man. It was a strong staff upon which to lean, a shield to hold against temptation.

The text used is one of memory, for without that memory who could know of the "glorious honor" of our Lord's majesty and of his wondrous works? And without a well-stored mind none can declare his goodness. It is only through personal experience that one can sing of his righteousness, for it comes through remembrance of that working power and what it has done in our individual lives—for what it has done for us in times of stress.

In childhood memories what treasures are absorbed, and from there to be called up at will! Within the tender convolutions of a child's brain beautiful and unforgettable experiences make their deep and lasting impressions. Especially is it so when, in those early years, the Christ is lifted up before that child. Then does he draw him with unbreakable and unchafable cords, cords that will hold firm a lifetime through.

To make a memory in any heart is a privilege and a responsibility. Some word we say, some kindly deed we do, some loving touch when the heart is sore will live on in memory like a steady lifted light. It behooves us to say the right word, to do the kindly deed, to be gentle in our touch, if these things are to become a living monument to us.

Long ago a minor poet, whose name has been lost in the dust of the years, wrote these words:

> When I am dead, the years will come and go
> As they do now. The words I've said
> When cares have vexed me so,
> Not thinking how words cling and cling to
> life
> Will still live on, when I am dead.
>
> While I am here I would live well the life
> I cannot keep, that in the years ahead
> When I have ceased the strife
> And sweetly sleep, some good will live
> Because I've been, though I am dead.

This beautiful, brief poem could be memorized with profit by each of us. It possibly might stay the tongue through vexing times;

it might wake a stronger desire to live better, more thoughtful lives. So in my heart I thank the poet who has long since "ceased the strife," for having thus set her heart down on paper.

I would like, if I may, to tell here of one particular memory I have held in my heart for long years. It shines there as does new silver in the high noon's light, and it does not dim with the passing of time. It is a strangely perpetual memory, for it comes to me often like beautiful, distant music.

When I was a young girl, I lived in a far northern state with my people. Our home was a rambling farm house set in the midst of apple and plum orchards that sent their swooning fragrance over the land in the spring. Our acreage lay at the very edge of a friendly little village, and every evening at sunset a bell, set high in a tall, climbing steeple, would peal forth its bright, silvery call to prayer—a call so clear and high and sweet that it could not fail to be heard and heeded.

The village folk would stop their labor for a while and bow their heads in humble worship. Crystal-clear came the sound. And young as I was, I would stop whatever task I might be

70

doing, or any game I was playing, and my heart would thrill at that high, insistent call. I, too, would pray a simple, sincere prayer, thus remembering God reverently and gratefully.

Often now in the crowded, clamoring city in which I live, I long to catch the sound of that sunset bell calling a people to prayer.

Sometimes, there in the golden dust of the streets, I think I can hear it—the sharp clear bugle notes cleaving the air—and I breathe a prayer at its imaginary call.

Perhaps there are thousands praying with me in that sunset moment, as they think of the day's work ended, and feel earnestly the need of God in their lives. I trust that this is so, even though there is no echoing bell voicing its silver call.

The heart has a blessed way of holding brightness in memory. Often the hard experiences through which we pass are forgotten as one forgets pain when it is past. It is good to remember only the joyous, happy moments of life.

It is especially good to hold in memory our Lord and his words, to recall through times of trial that "hitherto" he has helped and that he will help again. If we listen, we can hear his voice speaking across the years: "This do in remembrance of me." And so we partake of his broken body and his blood and arise better fitted to meet life and its perplexities. God grant that we may lay hold of "whatsoever things are true, whatsoever things are honest, whatsoever things are just, whatsoever things are pure, whatsoever things are of good report" and, storing them in memory, make beautiful our living.

Who Stores Bright Memories

He who has stored bright memories in his heart
Need never walk entirely alone,
Need never feel dismayed when days are dark,
For there are joys which he alone has known
That will light with flame the pathway that he
    takes
To guide him safely on his upward climb:
Memories undimmed by recent scenes
And untarnished by the brush of passing time.

Oh, hold them close! Oh, cherish them, my heart,
And bring them forth when days are cold and
    bleak!
They will warm you with a hearth fire's ruddy
    glow.
Old days will live again, old voices speak,
And youth itself, for which your heart may yearn,
That you thought lost forever, will return.

9

STEWARDSHIP

> *And the Lord said, Who is that faithful and wise steward, whom his lord shall make ruler over his household, to give them their portion of meat in due season? Blessed is that servant, whom his lord when he cometh shall find so doing.* LUKE 12:42-43

IN THIS LIFE WE ARE ENTRUSTED WITH POSSESsions that are not ours to keep. This business in living should be dealt with according to our Lord's teachings.

There are various kinds of stewardships other than that referred to in the above text. There is the tithing of our incomes, the sharing of our time, our love, our sympathetic understanding with others. It is a trust given us to keep conscientiously in a manner that will be pleasing to our Lord.

We think of time and of our stewardship of

that commodity. We recall how Jesus spent his earthly days. How simply it is stated: "He went about doing good." He was a steward for his Father. He went quietly about his day's work. He ever walked softly. One cannot imagine him wasting vital energy and strength in unnecessary haste; but so long were his hours, the demands upon him so incessant, that virtue went out of him to others in his healing ministry as he selflessly gave of his life's forces. He used his time meticulously and gave forth power far in excess of the tithe of his time and strength.

Those forces had to be renewed, and he regained them by slipping away to spend long hours in communion with his Father on some quiet hillside. From that contact he came forth immeasurably strengthened for his ministry among the poor and needy who desperately sought him for his healing touch, his magnetic personality.

When we think of time, the emphasis is not always on action. If the Lord required renewal in some secluded spot where he could be alone with God, how much more do we need it before we attempt any definite service for our fellow men? As Christian stewards should we not often take time to be alone with our heavenly Father? Should we not listen attentively to his directing voice? Should we not always ask for his wisdom that we may know how he desires us to spend the immediate hours ahead and for what service he deems us to be best fitted?

Not often can we reach the solitude of a mountainside, but there is the closet he has bidden us enter, and there is the door to close upon that quiet while of communion. Thus we can find God, and from there we can come forth with a clearer vision than we have had hitherto. We will be better able to see the far reaches of the fields that are white already with harvest, and, God grant, we may face our assigned tasks with willing heart and hands, ever alert to the human needs about us.

There is the stewardship of love. The Lord is very emphatic about the emotion called love. "Thou shalt love the Lord thy God with all thy heart, and with all thy soul, and with all thy strength, and with all thy mind; and thy neighbour as thyself," he says, and throughout the centuries this admonition has not been changed by a word.

We have been given hearts that are capable of

a great, holy, and lasting love. The Lord asks for his share, and we give it to him freely and gladly, for to whom else do we owe so great a debt?

We love others, for he has taught us the way through his vast compassion, his spirit of forgiveness, his boundless sympathy where hearts are sorely troubled.

We are stewards of our own income, be it large or small. Conscientiously, we should set aside God's allotted amount. We should keep books on his account. We have no more right to fail to pay him his just dues than to fail to pay any fellow man to whom we are indebted.

He loaned us life; he loaned us all the good and glorious things that seemingly are our possessions, and we must surely pay him the interest on that loan.

He is not a hard taskmaster. He does not require exorbitant interest, and he holds out glowing promise to all who will meet their obligations to him. "Try me and see," he says. His word is sure. His promises do not fail. All those who take him at his word are abundantly rewarded. "Try me and see," his voice sounds hearteningly across the centuries.

Bring ye all the tithes into the storehouse, . . . and prove me now herewith, saith the Lord of hosts, if I will not open you the windows of heaven, and pour you out a blessing, that there shall not be room enough to receive it.   (Mal. 3:10.)

Shall we not put him to the test? Shall we not religiously tithe all our resources? God grant that we be willing and cheerful stewards on our heavenward journey.

God's Steward

I am God's steward; I am nothing more,
And since he deems me worthy of his trust,
How watchful and how guarded I should be
As a good and faithful steward . . . Oh, I must
Not fail the One who thus has honored me,
Bidding me serve him daily at my best.
I pray for wisdom that I may do well
Each small appointed task at his behest.

I pray that I may reach an aiding hand
To help some brother struggling up a hill
Too steep for his lost strength. I pray I may
Be given the right words to speak that will
Bring comfort to a heart bereft and sad,
Thus as a steward, making others glad.

10

THE PRIVILEGE OF PRAYER

> *O thou that hearest prayer, unto thee shall*
> *all flesh come.*   PS. 65:2

THERE IS NO GREATER PRIVILEGE ALLOTTED TO
mankind than this boundless privilege of prayer.
What would the heart do without it? How lost
on the seas of time we would be if we did not
possess this anchor for the soul!

"Unto thee shall all flesh come." This is a
truth too vital to be ignored. The saint and the
sinner alike come to God: the saint at all times,
the sinner in his desperation, when hope seems
lost and there is nowhere else to go, will invari-
ably turn to a power that is greater than his own.
He will come, a craven, pleading for mercy to
the only true source of mercy and forgiveness.

The stanchest agnostic, when the time comes
that he must die, will turn his frightened, be-

wildered eyes skyward and cry for help from a sadly neglected God.

"O thou that hearest prayer." All men in time will turn to God from the uttermost parts of the earth. They will come as soon as men fully heed the admonition to "go tell" and the lost ones hear of his compassion and love for them.

We pray, but too often we pray at random. We are told definitely to make our request known as we come to God, and if they be according to his will, those requests will be answered. Many of us are not eloquent in prayer, but the great understanding heart of God makes ample allowances for our shortcomings.

I know of one dear, saintly woman who was very ill, and she bemoaned the fact that she was unable to pray as she longed to do. A Christian friend sat at her bedside and, with infinite wisdom and understanding, told her not to grieve, that the Lord understood, and he was not saying to her at that time to "be strong" but to "be still." "Now," she said, "is the time to trust. You are God's sick child, and he has his arms around you—and truly all he wants you to do is to rest and to trust him." And the ill one was helped and comforted by that sane advice. She

heeded it, and God worked mightily in her be-
half.

Many of us could learn to pray more acceptably if it were not for the clamor of the world
about us. We have our Lord's beautiful prayer
as an example of how to shape our petitions and
our praise. It is a wise, all comprehensive prayer
that covers well our human needs. Too often
our prayers are begging prayers rather than
those of adoration and praise, which would be
far more acceptable to our Lord. Yet we may
be certain he hears and heeds all earnest, sincere
prayers and pleadings and grants our hearts'
desires if he knows them to be best for us.

Perhaps the Indian sage and poet, Tagore, has
expressed best what factors should enter into
our praying. His humble petitions, his wise requests, must be indeed pleasing to a listening
God. His prayer runs thus:

Let me not pray to be sheltered from dangers, but
to be fearless in facing them; let me not pray for the
stilling of my pain, but for the heart to conquer it;
let me not look for allies in my life's battlefield; but
to my own strength; let me not crave in anxious
fear to be saved, but hope for the patience to win my
freedom. Grant me that I might not be a coward,

feeling your mercy in my success alone; but let me find the grasp of your hand in my failure.

This is prayer at its highest and noblest—a beautiful lofty petition that should help us all to better express our own hearts' desires through the storms of life.

From Jas. 1:5 we have this clearly expressed statement and assurance: "If any of you lack wisdom, let him ask of God, that giveth to all men liberally, and upbraideth not; and it shall be given him."

Who of us in times of frustration and bewilderment do not feel the lack of wisdom? How may we know what to ask for as we pray? The heart of our prayers should be a cry for that wisdom in our dealings with our fellow men, in our management of our own affairs. It is blessed to know that we have the promise that it will be given us without the "upbraiding" of our Heavenly Father because of our lack of knowledge. This statement alone should encourage us to praise the Lord and to ask for great things, great blessings, great mercies, and above all to praise him acceptably.

Humbly, we think of the Almighty One listening to our faltering, human petitions, not chiding us for any lack but willing to grant each reasonable request and more than pleased to accept our heartfelt adoration. Surely, we should be humble indeed before this stupendous fact.

Worship the Lord

"Worship the Lord in the beauty of holiness,"
The music wells upward where great choirs sing,
Bidding earth's people rejoice and adore him:
The Saviour of mankind, our Lord and our King.

In the white beauty of holiness worship.
Be reverent in praise of the dear Holy One;
Be earnest in praying the prayers that lift skyward
To honor and glorify God's precious Son.

"Worship the Lord in the beauty of holiness,"
Let nothing disturb that blest hour of prayer;
Let nothing unholy detract from the splendor
Of pure selfless worship set loose on the air.

11

SIMPLICITY

> *"Remember this, that very little is needed to make a happy life."*
>
> MEDITATIONS OF MARCUS AURELIUS

HERE IS ADMONITION WORTH HEEDING. SHOULD we do so, much of the fret and confusion of our day would be eliminated. Wealth and the possession of "things" do not make for happiness. On the contrary they may become a burden too great to be borne.

It is possible in our lives, even in these days of turmoil, to live simply, to walk softly, to keep heart and mind tranquil, and to live peaceably with our kind.

It will require strict discipline, for the world is too much with us. Its distractions are many, but the discipline will be worth while, for then —and then only—will there be time to cultivate the things of the spirit that are so vital to our daily living.

Our Lord lived simply. His food was simple: an occasional broiled fish, a bit of wild honey, a cupful of milk, at times a fig or so, when they could be found, and always clear water for his drink. His garments were simple: a loose robe and well-worn sandals. He had the sky for a roof, the horizons for his walls, the good earth for his footstool.

If we are to strive to be Christlike, it behooves us to be rid of much of the clutter in our lives. If he, the heir to the heavenly kingdom, could simplify his living, surely we should endeavor to do so.

Simplicity, even austerity, may bring freedom from care and often may bring that best of all possessions of the human heart: contentment.

There is a beautiful interior painted by a great artist that all but takes the breath of the earnest observer. It is a picture of a quaint, clean living room of long ago—a spring afternoon in Normandy, with light flooding goldenly through windows. There are only the simple necessities of life in the furnishings of that little room. There is a fireplace with a Bible and a few pewter plates on the broad mantel. There is a clock upon the wall pointing to the hour of five. A plain wooden chair is drawn close to a western window, and a woman sits there holding a baby in her arms. The sunlight sifts through the panes, shedding its glory upon their faces.

There is great peace and tranquility looking out from the mother's eyes that is restful to behold. The whole world of deep content is there. She has her plain, clean home, her child, and doubtless, a good man coming home at the supper hour. What more could she want?

One, in these days of overmuch, might find it in the heart to envy her. There are so many useless things in many homes, so many cares because of the clutter and confusion of our days. We need, and we cannot do without, the Bible. We need it ever near at hand for wisdom and strength. We require plates for the serving of our daily bread, and we must have the clock to point out the hour that we may do our simple tasks and then find rest in a home-sweet atmosphere.

The mother needs the child, and the child desperately needs a mother—her wise guidance, her

Christlike love. No one is truly poor who has God to go to for wisdom and strength.

Coarse, brown bread and a cup of tea—a natural hunger is far better than an over-full plate of expensive delicacies with a jaded appetite. A plain room furnished simply can be much more restful than one overlaid with plush hangings where the fresh, clean air of heaven is shut out.

Our times are such that we may all soon be called upon to observe the strictest economy. It would be well to accustom ourselves to simple living that we may meet that time undismayed —to meet it in the spirit of adventure, remembering that very little, after all, is needed to make a happy life.

I Would Live Simply

I would live simply; I would keep a space
Within my life, uncluttered, Lord, and free,
Where you can find a calm abiding place
Should you desire to come and dwell with me.
I would be quiet, for with you as guest
I need to listen to your every word,
To gain a wider vision, and to rest
Within your calming presence, blessed Lord.

I would live simply lest the press of things,
So prone to hurt, should turn my guest away.
I shall endeavor that no hour brings,
As hitherto, demands that spoil my day.
O come, dear Lord, come and abide with me,
And teach me the value of simplicity.

12

GOD'S GIFT OF LIFE

Thou hast granted me life and favour, and thy visitation hath preserved my spirit.
JOB 10:12

IT IS GOD WHO GIVES US OUR VERY EXISTENCE. He gives us the means of life through his continual, providential care. He gives us pure air to breathe, clear water to drink, the food we eat. He gives us the sky for a roof, the earth for a temporary home. It is only through his influences that the life of any of us is preserved. It is in him we live and move and have our being.

What an amazing thing is life! Only an almighty God could have conceived of it for his children. We are entrusted with a gift so rare, so marvelous, so splendid that we should think always of its intrinsic value, its vital worth, and live at our highest and best at all times.

Our Lord says, "I am come that they might have life, and that they might have it more abundantly." "They" means you, and it means me.

He had a great and a grave purpose in his coming to earth that far-off day. That coming has a direct bearing on your life and on mine. He came that we might live more abundantly than we would do were it not for his restraining power and helpful purpose. It is only through knowledge of him and his word that we may truly live the more abundant life.

We recall one life that was truly lived abundantly. Let us listen to what Paul says in regard to his own gift of life. He was suffering greatly in his ministry at the time, yet he cries out: "As sorrowful, yet always rejoicing; as poor, yet making many rich; as having nothing, and yet possessing all things." (2 Cor. 6:10.)

Paul's life was strangely paradoxical at all times. It was a life darkened by many adverse circumstances, yet it shines today across our pathway like rays of sunlight streaming through a dark wood.

Paul was sorrowful, he says. He was often completely destitute of life's necessities and its comforts, yet he rejoiced continually, having the consciousness of God's presence and of the glorious assurance of immortality.

He was poor in worldly goods, yet so on fire was he with his message of salvation for others that he made many rich in new-born faith, in trust, and in hope that they had not experienced before.

He had nothing—being one of the poorest of men as far as worldly wealth was concerned— yet he shouts out that he possessed all things. He had that most vital possession: a contented spirit, and having that, he truly possessed all things. How pleasing that abundant life must have been to God; how satisfying must have been this man, salvaged, as he had been from the evil of his former days, and promoted to a glorious life servitude by the most high God!

To live life at its best, one can only accomplish this by striving most earnestly to be more Christlike. We find his instructions for that type of living in the following verse:

He hath shewed thee, O man, what is good; and what doth the Lord require of thee, but to do justly, and to love mercy, and to walk humbly with thy God. (Mic. 6:8.)

If we do this, all the problems of life will be solved, and the answers will fall into line. God planned for our days to be beautiful, even under the poorest and most humble circumstances.

Away back in the early part of the last century, Alice Cary, an excellent poet, wrote a haunting, unforgettable poem that has a bearing upon life lived at its best. She titled it "The Last Hour."

It is a long poem, too long to quote in its entirety, but I would like to pass on to others a part of it that has meant much to me through the years. Perhaps many others know the poem, and if they do, they recognize, as I do, the poet's devotion and unfaltering faith in the Heavenly Father's will, his wise guidance of a consecrated life. A portion of the poem follows:

"If I were told that I must die tomorrow,
That the next sun
Which shines should bear me out beyond all
                      fear and sorrow
For anyone,
All the fight fought, all the short journey through,
What should I do?
I do not think that I would shrink or falter,
But just go on,

Doing my work, nor change, nor seek to alter
Aught that is gone,
But rise and move and love and smile and pray
For one more day.

.   .   .   .

But if a wondrous hand from the blue yonder
Held out a scroll
On which my life was writ, and I with wonder
Beheld unroll
To a long century's end, its mystic clew,
What should I do?
What could I do, O blessed Lord and Master,
Other than this:
Still to go on, not slower and not faster,
Nor fear to miss
The road, how very long it be
While led by thee?

Here is the abundant life pictured beautifully and helpfully in poetry. I feel sure that the
dear poet, long gone to her eternal reward, would
not mind my quoting her for the good of others,
I feel I can do so with her unqualified blessing.

The Upward Climb

O, Hearts, with our faces lifted
To the high blue arc of the sky,
Let us have strong faith for our journey
And a star to guide us by
As we start on our upward climbing
Into rarer, purer air.
Our soul's supreme adventure
Will surely await us there.

For God's own hand will open
New vistas for our sight,
New summits for our conquest,
And for our minds new light
Upon life with its glorious purpose
And the importance of our time—
O, Hearts, with the strength God gives us,
Let us staunchly make the climb.

13

OUR CHANGELESS FRIEND

> *Henceforth I call you not servants; for the servant knoweth not what his lord doeth; but I have called you friends; for all things that I have heard of my Father I have made known unto you.* JOHN 15:15

THE GREATEST SPIRITUAL POSSESSION ANY heart can claim is the changeless and eternal friendship of the Christ. He himself has summed up the magnitude of that devotion when he says, "Greater love hath no man than this, that a man lay down his life for his friends."

This he most certainly did for us that day on Calvary, thus proving his love, his pity, his everlasting friendship for mankind—for you and for me.

We recall that once our Lord made an amazing statement to his followers. He told them that hitherto he had called them servants, but now he was admitting them to intimate fellowship with himself, and that he was willing to impart to them the things he had learned in his close association with his Father.

He told them that he had called them to be his disciples, to be witnesses to the truths he would teach them, and that he had ordained them to go out and bring in good fruit for his kingdom. Then as a glorious reward for their faithfulness, he told them that whatsoever they would ask the Father in his name, it would be granted them.

Thus between them and their Lord there was a beautiful friendship, established for time and for eternity.

It is a heartening and a reassuring fact to remember that his friendship extends much farther than to his disciples of old. We, too, are linked in that friendship with unbreakable links, for did he not, in almost the last prayer he uttered while here on the earth, all but call us by name? Did he not pray for those who would believe on him through his word, those who had received the assurance of his undying friendship? We believe, and, therefore, we have his word that we shall have his proved friendship forever. What a privilege! What an inestimable blessing!

Webster tells us the word "friend" is part of a verb meaning to love (as frēond). He also says it means one attracted to another by esteem, respect, and affection. Jesus says, "I have called you friends."

Think of what it means to have his esteem, his high regard, his respect! Does it not mean that he deems us worthy, in a way, of his affection and of his tender and zealous attachment?

The enemies of Jesus found fault with him because they said he was a friend of sinners—which he was. It became his chief distinction later on that he was known as a friend of the outcast, the weak, and the poor, the sinful and the unfortunate.

Someone has said that the one great sign of a man's greatness and nobility is how much he has befriended those in need of a friend.

Our Lord was a friend of the leper. The piteous cry, "unclean," ringing out across the bleak landscape did not deter him. He went straight and fearlessly to the one sorely afflicted. He placed his hands upon him and bade him, "be clean," and he was clean.

He was a friend to the blind, staying his course as he moved through the throng to open those eyes to the glory of a hitherto unseen day. He responded to the cry of all who were "grievously tormented." In fact we are told over and over that "he had compassion on the multitude." He was their friend. He is our friend today.

Did he not state clearly the meaning of true friendship when he said:

Come ye blessed of my Father, inherit the kingdom prepared for you from the foundation of the world: For I was an hungered, and ye gave me meat: I was thirsty, and ye gave me drink: I was a stranger, and ye took me in. Naked, and ye clothed me: I was sick, and ye visited me: I was in prison, and ye came unto me.   (Matt. 25:34-36.)

This is truly the Lord's conception of vital friendship. He tells us that if we have done these things unto the least of these his brethren, his friends, we have done it unto him.

It is a marvelous privilege that we are enabled to serve him in this our world today— our poor, troubled, bewildered world! If we think earnestly of it, it is our Lord yonder, begging for help on the street corner. It is our friend who is ill in the hospital or lying lonely in the nursing home.

It was Jesus who came hungry and thirsty to our door. He is the cloakless man, shivering out in the cold. If we have two coats, should we not give him one of them?

Shall we not share our roof, our loaf, our glowing fire with our Lord, since all the needy ones are he? Shall we not, to the best of our ability, have something of the same compassion for others as he had, and thus be fitted, later on, to share the kingdom of heaven with our friend, the son and heir of God?

I Have Called You Friends

"I have called you friends," a clear, high, clarion
    call
That sounds across the centuries today
Rings out as true as when he spoke the words
To those who walked beside him on the way.
Oh, beautiful the meaning of the words!
Oh, hearts be worthy of the sacred name
Of Friend, when uttered by the Lord of Hosts!
Lay hold of it, and warm you by its flame.

Go seek him out, this true and faithful one;
Tell him your heart's deep need, your soul's desire,
And he will answer. To what greater goal
Could any earnest seeking heart aspire
Than this, to know that to the journey's end
You will have as a companion this true friend.

14

THE ULTIMATE TRIUMPH

---

*Who is among you that feareth the Lord
. . . that walketh in darkness, and hath no
light? let him trust in the name of the Lord,
and stay upon his God.*   ISA. 50:10

OUR LORD DOES NOT ASK THE IMPOSSIBLE OF
any of his children. In our make-up as individuals he has given us an inner strength
which he supplies in time of need. He has promised us this strength for our days, a strength
which may not have been tested hitherto but
will hold if we but trust him enough, and if
we stay our minds confidently upon him through
any difficult experience.

Life often brings many blinding things. As
we listen, there is a stirring like the brush of
wings, as countless thousands pass by on the
earthly roads. They are walking in the darkness
of sorrow, of suffering, of poverty, of seeming

defeat. They go seeking for light; they are straining toward it with tear-blinded eyes and groping hands, and all the while above them sounds the pleading, compassionate voice of our Lord bidding them to trust him, to stay their minds upon him. Blessed, ah, blessed indeed are they who listen and heed that wise admonition!

God knows the dark depths of human sorrow and suffering. He understands our feeble frames, our shortsightedness, he sees the end while we but see the way, and he knows that out of darkness will come light.

Did he not watch the agony of his own son on the cross? There is no suffering for a parent as difficult to bear as that of seeing one's own child writhing under the torment of pain.

God understands our sorrow, for we are made in his image and his heart is like our hearts. He mourns with us as we mourn, and his compassion for us is boundless.

The following incident sheds light upon what grief can mean to a human heart. We are told that Queen Victoria, in the early days of her widowhood, cried out to an understanding friend: "I am always reaching out to consult one who is not here, groping by myself with a constant sense of desolation." Truly "a constant sense of desolation" accurately describes the darkness of the soul after the loss of a loved one, but God, in his infinite mercy, points out the light ahead. "Trust me—stay your minds on me," he says, "and your grief will lessen as time passes, under my merciful provision for you."

Amy Carmichael, the eminent English writer, tells in her beautiful book, *Gold by Moonlight*, of a crisis in the life of Amiel, that great and good man of another century, of whom it was said that he ever came to his desk as to an altar, so deeply conscious was he always of God's abiding presence. Amiel knew intimately the darkness of suffering—the long, hard days, the seemingly endless nights. One day he was told by his doctors that he could not survive the illness under which he was laboring. It came to him at first as a dreadful shock.

"On waking," he said, "it seemed to me I was staring into the future with wide startled eyes. Is it indeed to me that these things apply: my slavery becoming heavier, my circle of activities steadily narrowing, all possibilities being closed one by one?"

Being human, he questioned; he feared. For

a time he even doubted the goodness of God, but he who had walked so long in the light found it again as his ultimate triumph.

"One word is worth all others," he cried. "Thy will, not mine, be done." And he wrote at last in his diary these words, radiant with meaning: "To will what is God's will, brings peace."

But oh, we say, can it be God's will that anyone should suffer, should sorrow, should go groping in darkness? The answer comes: "Trust in me, stay upon me." And even though now we see through a glass but darkly, some day, with the light of heaven shining in our eyes, all things will be made plain, and we will then praise God even for the hardships we may have endured on our earthly journey, since he in his infinite wisdom permitted them to shadow our days.

Could it not be that our Lord allows some of his children to bear the burden of suffering or sorrow in order to enable them to go to others in understanding sympathy? Could it possibly be an honor conferred upon certain ones he feels he can trust to go on these errands of mercy?

How bewildered and lost would that one afflicted be if no other one had ever gone that rough way before! If no one could understand or could bring the comfort and encouragement of a shared experience!

Thank God, thank God, that even on the darkest road of life there is the certainty of ultimate triumph of good, of victory through seeming defeat, if we but heed his voice and walk in the light of his word!

The Trusting Heart

A trusting heart is one that does not doubt,
Though storms are threatening and all about
Are evil tidings loosed upon the air.
The trusting heart knows well his God is there:
A loving Father, understanding friend,
A companion for him to the journey's end,
His arms about him with a love so great
That the darkest path will brighten, soon or late.

The trusting heart in life's hard school has learned
To wait the answering voice for which it yearned.
And because that heart has heeded and has stayed
Upon its God, it need not be afraid.
O blessed, blessed peace that surely must
Reward all those who fully, freely trust.